# «DINOSAURS» DOWN UNDER

## AND OTHER FOSSILS FROM AUSTRALIA

## BY CAROLINE ARNOLD

### Photographs by
### RICHARD HEWETT

CLARION BOOKS

New York

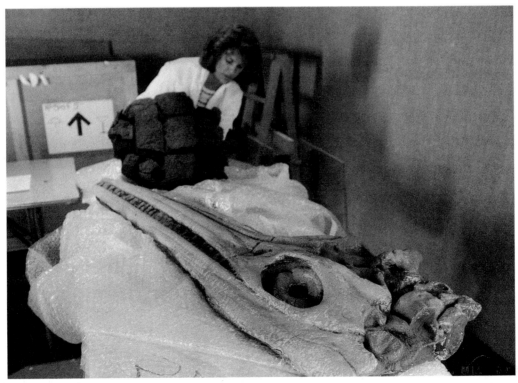

*For Ann Troy*

*With love from Caroline and Dick*

Clarion Books
a Houghton Mifflin Company imprint
215 Park Avenue South, New York, NY 10003
Text copyright © 1990 by Caroline Arnold
Photographs copyright © 1990 by Richard Hewett
All rights reserved.

For information about permission to reproduce
selections from this book, write to Permissions,
Houghton Mifflin Company, 2 Park Street, Boston, MA 02108.

Printed in Italy

**Library of Congress Cataloging-in-Publication Data**
Arnold, Caroline.
Dinosaurs down under : and other fossils from Australia /
by Caroline Arnold ; photographs by Richard Hewett.
p.   cm.
Includes index.
Summary: Text and photographs describe how a museum exhibit,
on loan from Australia, is shipped, assembled, and displayed
in a Los Angeles museum. Discusses the unique fossils of
prehistoric Australian creatures.
ISBN 0-89919-814-7
1. Dinosaurs — Australia — Juvenile literature.   2. Paleontology —
Australia — Juvenile literature.   3. Museum techniques — Juvenile
literature.   [1. Dinosaurs — Australia.   2. Paleontology — Australia.
3. Museum methods.]   I. Hewett, Richard, ill.   II. Title.
QE862.D5A753   1989
566′.0994 — dc20      89-32783
CIP
AC

NWI 10 9 8 7 6 5 4 3 2 1

# ACKNOWLEDGMENTS

This book focuses on the exhibit *Kadimakara: Fossils of the Australian Dreamtime*, assembled by the Queen Victoria Museum and Art Gallery, Launceston, Tasmania, which was on view at the Natural History Museum of Los Angeles County from April 9 through June 26, 1988.

Many people helped us with this project, and we want to extend our appreciation to all of them. We especially thank Professor Pat Rich, Monash University, Melbourne, Australia, who helped organize the Kadimakara exhibit and who provided valuable information for the manuscript as well as expert advice. We could not have done this book without the cooperation of the people at the Natural History Museum of Los Angeles County. In particular, we want to thank Ellen Girardeau, Public Relations, for her inspiration and for coordinating the many necessary arrangements. We also thank Heather Northway, Ronald Sabados, Barbara Allen, Mark Cattanach, Jan Davidson, and all the other members of the museum staff who assisted us while the exhibit was being installed. Lastly, we give special thanks to Anna Banghaman, Ernestine Frazier-Hinds, Belissa Martin, Brandon Frazier, Rocky Hinds II, Linda and Sasha Sircus, Austin Skelman, Oliver Shute, and Jennifer Arnold for their cheerful assistance with the photographs.

**H**idden by leaves, a pair of huge reptilian eyes peered out of the underbrush near the edge of a small water hole. Suddenly, the giant lizard's body tensed as a smaller, furry animal emerged on the opposite side of the clearing. The thirsty animal slowly moved toward the water and lowered its head to drink. In a swift motion, the giant lizard leaped from its hiding place, dug its sharp teeth and claws into the furry animal's skin, and quickly killed it.

If you were living in Australia 100,000 years ago, you might easily have witnessed such a scene. Today, however, there are no giant lizards. They and their prey are extinct, and most of the water holes they drank from are dry. What we know about these animals and the world they lived in comes from studying their fossilized bones and other evidence from the past.

*Left: Bone fragments of* Siderops, *an ancient salamander-like animal.*
*Right: Dinosaur footprint.*

Scientists believe that the earliest forms of life appeared on earth about 3.5 billion years ago. These were simple, tiny organisms that gradually evolved into a wide variety of much more complex plants and animals. In Australia, as elsewhere, most of the ancient life forms lived and died and left no remains. Sometimes, however, parts of these organisms were preserved as fossils. A fossil may be any part of a plant or animal that is preserved in some way, or it may be an impression, such as a footprint or leaf print, made by a living organism.

Fossils are found in all kinds of places — on mountains, along rivers, in rock quarries, where roads are being built, or in excavations for new buildings. Sometimes fossils are found by chance, but more often they are discovered by people who know where to look for them. These people who study fossils are called paleontologists. They identify fossils by comparing them with other fossils and with similar structures in modern life forms.

6

The first discoveries of Australian fossils were made by explorers in the 1830s. They found fossil bones of giant birds and strange kangaroo-like animals that lived thousands of years ago. In this century, paleontologists have discovered many more fossils, including those of dinosaurs and other animals that lived in Australia millions of years ago. Both fossils and the rocks in which they are preserved help scientists to understand what life used to be like on that continent.

By comparing Australian fossils with those found in other parts of the world, we can get a clearer picture of how life developed all over our planet. For instance, the similarity between dinosaur bones found in Australia and in other parts of the world provides evidence that the continents were once much closer together than they are now. Over millions of years, the continents have been slowly moving across the surface of the earth. In the dinosaur age, Australia was much farther south than it is today and was connected to Antarctica. At that time, the earth was much warmer than it is now so that Antarctica was not covered with ice, although it was still quite cool at high altitudes.

*Leaf fossil*

For most of us, the best way to see fossils is to go to a museum. Recently, an exhibit of Australian fossils traveled to Los Angeles, California, to be displayed at the Natural History Museum there. It was the first time that people in the United States had a chance to see such a large group of fossils from the land "down under."

The exhibit was called *Kadimakara: Fossils of the Australian Dreamtime*. The title of the exhibit refers to an ancient legend of the aborigines, the native people of Australia. The aborigines are believed to have migrated to Australia from Southeast Asia about 40,000 years ago, or possibly even earlier. Their lives centered around hunting, fishing, and gathering native fruits and vegetables. They believed that the world was created in a period of the distant past called dreamtime.

According to an aborigine legend, the center of Australia, which is now a vast, dry, mostly uninhabited desert, was once a lush garden filled with huge trees, water, and many different kinds of animals. In the treetops lived strange creatures called *Kadimakara*; each day these dreamtime creatures came down from the trees to look for food. One day, when the Kadimakara were on the ground, the trees they needed to climb back to their homes were destroyed. The Kadimakara were forced to remain on the ground, and there they died, leaving their bones to litter the earth. The animals represented by the fossils in the exhibit also died and left their bones behind. Unlike the mythical Kadimakara animals, the fossil animals were once real, and their bones help tell the story of what life might have been like long ago.

*Fossils of ancient plants provide clues to what the landscape was like.*

*A blueprint indicates where to put up exhibit panels.*

For months before the Kadimakara fossils came to Los Angeles, the museum staff prepared for their arrival. They wanted to be sure everything would be ready so that the exhibit could be installed quickly.

Because every exhibit is different, the people at the museum must design a special plan for each one. Before making the plan, the designer needs to know how many and what kind of items will be coming, how large the items are, and what rooms will be used. For the Kadimakara exhibit, the plan was to put everything in the center of a large room. There carpenters began to construct the platforms and display panels that would be needed.

One day news came that the fossils had arrived at the shipyard and would be delivered soon by truck. As the large wooden crates arrived at the museum's loading dock, they were carefully carried out of the truck and taken into the exhibit hall. Because a sudden change in temperature or humidity can damage exhibit items, especially those that are old or fragile, the crates remained unopened for several days. That way the fossils and other objects could slowly adjust to the air in the room. Then, at last, the lids were unfastened so everything could be unpacked.

*Left: The crates of fossils arrive at the museum. Below: A section of the giant lizard skeleton must be examined before it can be removed from its crate.*

*Left: Gloves are always worn when handling valuable objects to keep them as clean as possible. Above: Protective pads on the tables help keep items from becoming scratched or broken as they are unpacked.*

Inside the exhibit hall, tables had been set up for the workers to use as they unpacked the crates. As for each exhibit that came to the museum, the registrar was responsible for checking that everything had arrived safely. She made sure that all the items were included, that each was identified correctly, and that no damage had occurred during shipping.

As each item in the Kadimakara exhibit was unwrapped, the museum registrar examined it and found it on the list. Everything had to be checked carefully, and for this large exhibit, the process took several days. At the end of the show, when it was time to take down the exhibits, the registrar again checked each item before it was wrapped and packed for its return to Australia.

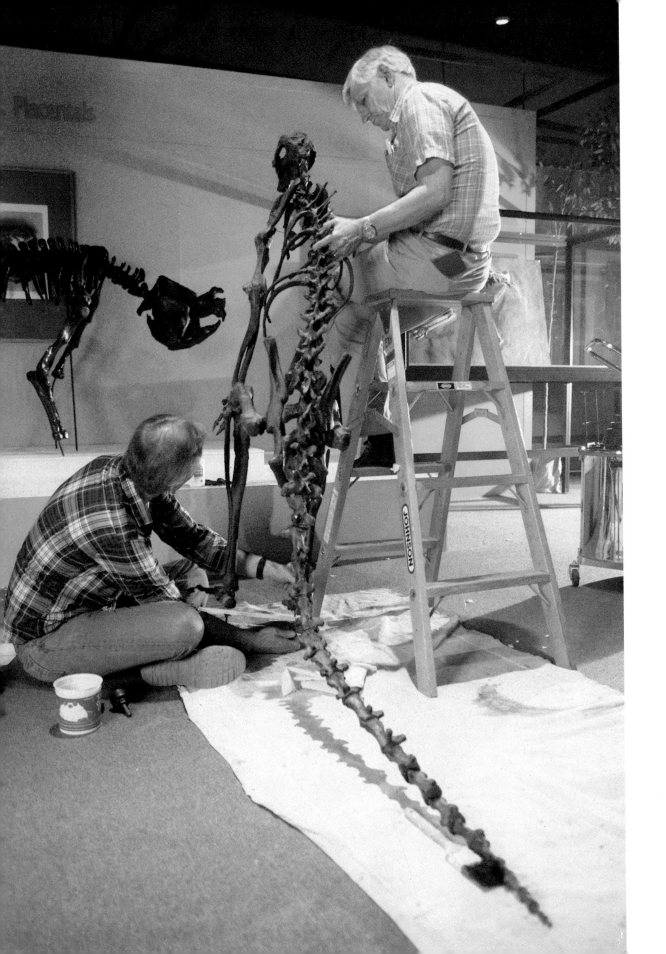

After the fossils were "logged in" by the registrar, they were put on display. Small items went into glass cases, large items were put on platforms, and paintings and signs were hung on panels.

People who work in the exhibits department at the museum are responsible for putting up and taking down all displays in the museum. If there is a question about an object, they may consult one of the specialists on the museum staff or another expert. Professionals may also come to study objects in the displays. While the Kadimakara exhibit was being installed, several of the museum's paleontologists came to carefully examine the fossils before they were locked into the display cases.

*Far left: If an item arrives at the museum damaged or broken, staff members may have to repair it before it can be displayed. Below left: The jawbone of a giant wombat, a large animal similar to a ground hog, is placed in a display case. Below right: The base of this skeleton is painted to match the exhibit platform.*

*Museum paleontologists assist in the assembly of this giant lizard skeleton.*

Some of the skeletons in the Kadimakara exhibit, including that of the giant lizard, were so big that they had been shipped in sections. After the sections were unpacked, they had to be brought to the exhibit platform and reassembled by the museum staff.

Like several of the other skeletons, that of the giant lizard was made not of fossils but of copies, or *casts*, of the actual fossil bones. Missing pieces were created by measuring bones in the skeletons of present-day lizards and enlarging them to fit. These casts and models are made from much lighter material and are easier to ship and work with than real fossil bones, which are actually rock. Casts also allow copies of one-of-a-kind skeletons or bones to be displayed while the original fossils are being used for study.

Before the Kadimakara fossils arrived, the museum staff had prepared signs to go with the exhibit. In addition, they used informational labels that had come with each of the items. After all the objects were installed in cases or on platforms, and all of the signs and labels were put in their correct places, the carpenters completed the platform railings. Then the lights were put up and adjusted, and the empty crates were removed. Finally, the Kadimakara exhibit was ready to open for the public.

*Maps and signs help visitors learn about the fossils in the exhibit.*

Bones of more than sixty different kinds of animals are represented in the Kadimakara exhibit. All of them are from members of the large group of animals called *vertebrates*, or animals with backbones. Vertebrates have internal bony skeletons that protect and support their bodies. Each small bone that is part of the backbone, or spine, is called a *vertebra*, which means "joint" in Latin. Humans have twenty-four vertebrae. You can feel your own vertebrae if you rub your hand along your spine.

The first backboned animals on earth were fish, and some of them, like the strange jawless fish called *Arandaspis* (air-an-DAS-pis), lived as early as 480 million years ago. In Australia, fossils of ancient fish show that the interior of that continent, now a vast desert, was often covered by shallow seas. There are a large number of well-preserved fish fossils in Australia. Some of the oldest are of fish covered with strange, bony plates. Other ancient fish had large, bony fins on their backs.

*Hundreds of fish were preserved when an ancient sea dried up 350 million years ago.*

Amphibians (am-FIB-ee-anz) form another group of vertebrates whose fossil remains have been found in Australia. Modern animals such as frogs and salamanders are amphibians. The word *amphibian* comes from two Greek words meaning "both lives" — these are animals that live both in water and on land. Amphibians often begin life in water, but, as adults, they breathe air with their lungs. They can also breathe underwater by absorbing oxygen through their skin. Amphibians were the first animals to have four feet.

Unlike their modern relatives, which are comparatively small animals, some of the ancient amphibians were huge. An unusual Australian amphibian that lived about 200 million years ago is called by its scientific name, *Siderops* (SIGH-der-ops). This animal was about 8 feet (2.4 meters) long and had a large, flat, shovel-shaped head. *Siderops* belongs to a group of large, crocodile-sized animals called labyrinthodonts (la-buh-RINTH-o-donts), whose name comes from Greek words that refer to the mazelike structure of the teeth. Nearly one hundred sharp teeth rimmed the wide mouth of *Siderops* and were used to catch the fish that it ate.

*Casts of fossil bones of* Siderops, *an amphibian that lived at the same time as the dinosaurs.*

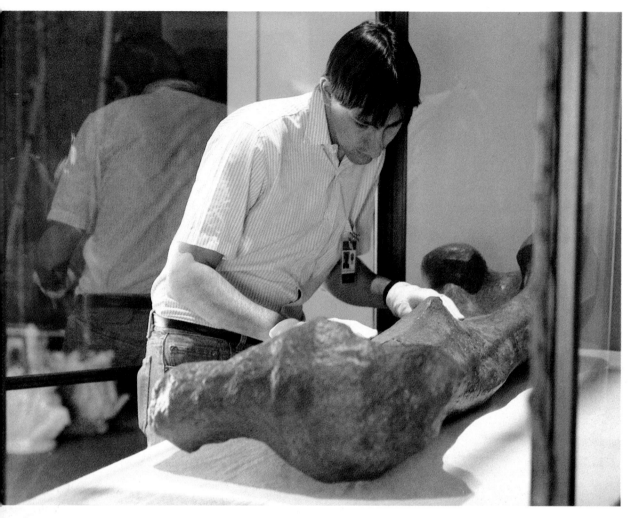

*Above: This cast of a giant Queensland dinosaur thigh bone is 5 feet (1.5 meters) long.  Far right: Model of a* Hypsilophodon *skeleton.*

The third group of vertebrates, and one of the most fascinating fossil groups, is that of the reptiles. The word *reptile* comes from a Latin word that means "creeping" or "crawling," which is how many reptiles move. Reptiles, like amphibians, are four-footed (except for snakes) and do not maintain a constant body temperature. However, reptiles can breathe only with their lungs, and their bodies are covered with tough, dry scales instead of smooth, moist skin. Reptiles either bear live young or lay eggs on land. Modern reptiles include snakes, lizards, crocodiles, alligators, turtles, and tortoises.

Among the early reptiles of Australia is the giant Queensland dinosaur. Bones of this enormous animal were first discovered in 1924. It lived about 180 million years ago and has been given the scientific name *Rhoetosaurus* (rho-to-SAWR-us), which means "giant lizard." *Rhoetosaurus* was a plant eater and a member of the sauropod (SAWR-uh-pod) or "lizard foot" group of dinosaurs, the largest animals ever to walk the earth. The giant Queensland dinosaur grew to be more than 50 feet (15 meters) long, and it resembled dinosaurs such as *Brontosaurus* (BRON-tuh-SOR-us), also known as *Apatosaurus* (ah-PAT-uh-SOR-us). These gigantic, long-necked, long-tailed creatures probably ate leaves from the tops of trees much like modern giraffes do.

*Hypsilophodon* (hip-suh-LAHF-uh-dahn), whose name means "high-crested tooth," was a small, plant-eating dinosaur that lived 135 to 100 million years ago. It was about 5 feet (1.5 meters) long and stood about 2 feet (.6 meters) high. It belonged to a group of dinosaurs called ornithopods (ORE-nith-uh-pods), meaning "bird feet," and could run quickly on its hind legs.

*Left: Reproduction of the belly armor of the* Minmi *dinosaur.*

One of the strangest looking of the Australian dinosaurs was the *Minmi* (MEN-mi), named after the place where it was found, Minmi Crossing in Queensland. The *Minmi* was about 12 feet (3.7 meters) long and covered with tough, armorlike skin that protected it from predators such as the meat-eating dinosaur *Allosaurus* (al-o-SAWR-us), which roamed much of the ancient world. The *Minmi* belongs to a dinosaur group called the ankylosaurs (an-KY-luh-sors). Different kinds of ankylosaurs are known to have lived in Europe and North America.

Another group of large reptiles that lived during the age of dinosaurs is called the ichthyosaurs (IK-thee-uh-sors), or "fish lizards"; they lived in the sea. Fossils of ichthyosaurs have been found in many places in Australia; some of these fossils are from animals more than

*A large head with a narrow snout was typical of a fish lizard.*

17 feet (5.6 meters) long. Although they were reptiles, the ichthyo-saurs looked very much like dolphins, which are mammals. Ichthyo-saurs lived their whole lives in the sea, where they ate fish and other small sea animals. Fossilized baby ichthyosaurs have been found in-side the fossil skeletons of females, which suggests that the "fish liz-ards" probably gave birth to live young.

The dinosaur age began about 245 million years ago and ended about 65 million years ago, when all of those giant creatures became extinct. However, other kinds of reptiles, such as crocodiles and liz-ards, did not die out. Among the more recent reptile species found as fossils in Australia is the giant goanna lizard, also known by its scien-tific name, *Megalania* (meg-a-LANE-ee-a), which means "the great ripper," after its method of killing prey.

*Megalania* roamed Australia during the last 2 million years, and, although it is now extinct, it was known and feared by the early aborigines. Like the present-day Komodo dragon lizards of Indonesia, *Megalania* was a large, meat-eating reptile.

Although only a few bones of *Megalania* have been found, paleontologists have been able to figure out what the complete skeleton

would probably be like by comparing the fossil bones to the skeletons of living goannas such as the 10-foot (3.2-meter) Komodo dragon. Scientists estimate that an adult *Megalania* was probably about 22 feet (7 meters) long and weighed more than 1,300 pounds (600 kilograms), making it the largest and one of the most dangerous animals on the Australian landscape of its time.

Birds are the fourth group of vertebrates represented in the Kadi-makara exhibit. Scientists believe that the earliest birds evolved from dinosaurs about 150 million years ago. Even today birds and reptiles share some of the same characteristics — they both have scaly legs, lay eggs, and have some similar bones in their skeletons. However, only birds have feathers, and, unlike living reptiles, they can maintain a constant body temperature. Fossils of extinct birds in Australia include those of giant penguins, flamingos, and a turkey-sized bird called the giant megapode. Fossil bones, eggshells, and footprints provide information about the appearance and behavior of these ancient birds.

Some of the most amazing of Australia's extinct birds are the mihirungs, whose name comes from aboriginal words meaning "giant emus." Emus, which stand about 4 feet (1.2 meters) tall, are large, flightless birds that live in Australia today. Mihirungs are a group of birds known on no other continent and include the heaviest bird ever to live. Named *Dromornis stirtoni* (droe-MOR-nis stir-TOE-nee) after its discoverer, R. A. Stirton, and two Greek words meaning "running bird," this bird was at least 10 feet (3.1 meters) tall and weighed nearly 1,100 pounds (500 kilograms). Fragments of fossil eggs that may have belonged to this giant bird have been found. If whole, these eggs would measure up to 16.5 inches (42 centimeters) long and have a volume of 3.2 gallons (12 liters), nearly ten times as large as the egg of a modern emu.

*Model of a giant egg belonging to a mihirung bird called* Aepyornis *(A-pee-OR-nis), meaning "high bird."*

At least eight species of mihirungs have lived in Australia during the past 15 million years. One of the more recent mihirung species, which has the scientific name *Genyornis* (jenny-OR-nis), may have been alive as late as 6,000 years ago. It is known to have lived at the same time as the early aborigines, and it is possible that *Genyornis* was hunted by them. Fossil skeletons of *Genyornis* have been found in several locations and indicate that it lived in small groups and inhabited both forests and grasslands. Like the present-day emu, *Genyornis* could not fly. However, it could run fast on its long legs and easily escape most predators.

*Left: Heavy leg bones and strong muscles helped the mihirungs to run fast.*

*Right: The skeleton of* Genyornis *resembles that of the modern ostrich.*

The fifth and last group of vertebrates is composed of the mammals, warm-blooded animals that have fur or hair and feed their babies milk. The word *mammal* comes from "mamma," the Latin word for breast. There are three kinds of mammals: *monotremes*, or those like the platypus that lay eggs; *marsupials*, or those like kangaroos that carry their babies in pouches; and *placentals*, or animals like dogs, cats, and humans, in which the female nourishes the young inside her womb until it is ready to be born. Mammals began to evolve during the age of di-

*This skeleton of a modern platypus is smaller than that of its now-extinct ancestor.*

nosaurs. The most primitive mammals laid soft-shelled eggs, similar to those of reptiles. Australia's oldest known mammal lived about 110 million years ago and resembled the present-day platypus. Like the platypus, it was a monotreme and had a ducklike snout that it used to find food along the stream beds where it lived. A young platypus drinks milk that oozes out of pores on the underside of its mother's belly — the young of this early mammal might have done the same. Only a few fossils of early monotremes have been found in Australia.

About 100 million years ago, the Australian continent began to separate from the other land masses to which it had been joined and became isolated from the rest of the world. Many unique forms of life developed in Australia. On other continents, placental animals evolved and gradually replaced the marsupials and monotremes, but in Australia, where there were no placental mammals, the marsupials developed to a very advanced level.

Australia is unusual in that it has a wider variety of marsupials, both past and present, than anywhere else in the world. Perhaps the best-known Australian marsupial is the kangaroo. As with other marsupials, the female gives birth to a baby when it is very small and at an early stage of development. The newborn kangaroo, called a *joey*, is only half an inch long and must crawl to its mother's pouch, where it remains for the next five to six months as it continues to grow.

Among the early, now extinct, relatives of the present-day kangaroo is a group called the *Protemnodons* (pro-TEM-no-donz). There were several species in this group, some of which grew much bigger than modern kangaroos. Like kangaroos today, the *Protemnodons* were plant eaters.

*Right: Extinct species such as this* Protemnodon *had longer necks, stronger forelimbs, and shorter hind limbs than modern kangaroos.*

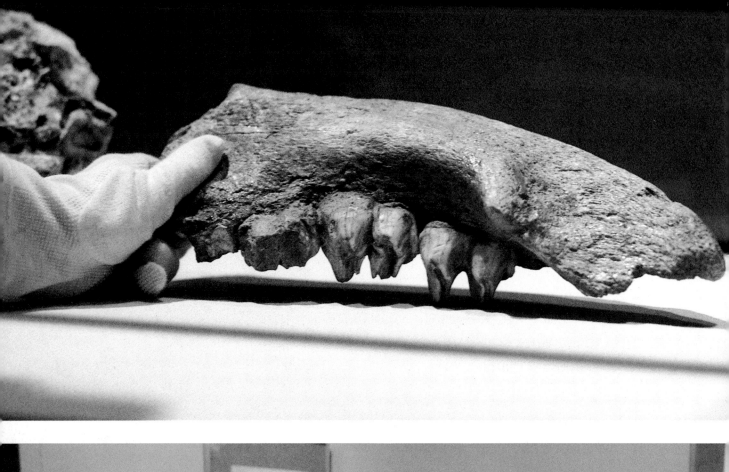

One of the amazing things about Australia's marsupials is that some of them are quite similar to placental animals on other continents. The largest known marsupial stood over 6 feet (1.8 meters) tall at the shoulders and looked something like a furry rhinoceros without horns. It was called *Diprotodon* (die-PRO-to-don), meaning "two forward teeth," and lived in Australia during the last 2 million years. It became extinct between 25,000 and 15,000 years ago. Fossil bones of this plant-eating animal have been found over much of Australia, and it may have been hunted by the early aborigines.

A dog-sized marsupial that roamed the forests of Australia 10 million years ago was called *Ngapakaldia* (nap-a-CALL-de-a), after the place where it was discovered, Lake Ngapakaldia. It traveled in herds and ate plants.

*Right: The flexible joints on the foot of* Ngapakaldia *may have been useful for climbing trees.*

*Top left: The ridged molar teeth of the* Diprotodon *were good for chewing leaves.*

*Below left:* Zygomaturus *(zy-go-ma-TOOR-us) was a slightly smaller relative of* Diprotodon *that lived on the island of Tasmania, as well as in the more humid parts of mainland Australia.*

Although most of the ancient Australian animals were plant eaters, there were a few meat eaters that preyed on them. One of these was the marsupial lion, whose scientific name is *Thylacoleo* (thigh-lack-o-LEO), meaning "pouched lion." In one nearly complete fossil skeleton, remnants of young lions were found where the animal's pouch would have been. Although somewhat smaller than a modern lion, it was nevertheless a fierce predator. The bones of *Thylacoleo* have been found along with those of kangaroos, suggesting that these animals may have been a major food source for the marsupial lion.

A species of marsupial lion called *Thylacoleo carnifex* lived during the last 2 million years. It became extinct about 18,000 years ago, at a time when the climate of Australia became very dry, and many of the plant-eating animals on which it depended for food died out.

*The marsupial lion had sharp teeth and claws good for killing and ripping apart its prey.*

Most Australian fossils have been discovered only in the last century and many in just the past twenty-five years. They reveal a fascinating history that is quite distinct from that of the rest of the world.

Fossils are our windows on the past. Through them we can learn about the ancient landscape, its climate, and what kinds of plants and animals inhabited it. Like animals all over the earth, those in Australia had to adapt as their environment changed. The earth we live on is constantly changing, and the more we can learn about the past, the better we will be able to anticipate the future.

# MOVING CONTINENTS

If you had been able to view the earth from outer space 500 million years ago, it would have looked very different from what astronauts see today. North America would appear to be tipped sideways and located mostly south of the equator. Australia would be north of the equator and part of a large landmass called Gondwanaland. Three hundred and fifty million years later, your outer-space view would show that Australia had moved south, and that North America was now joined to South America. The reason that we sometimes call Australia the land "down under" is because today it is in the Southern Hemisphere, and appears on the underneath half of the globe.

The study of how the continents move across the surface of the earth is called *plate tectonics*. According to the plate tectonics theory, the earth is made of melted rock covered by a hard outer layer called the earth's crust. Pieces of the crust, known as continental plates, slide over the melted rock below like parts of a giant, sphere-shaped jigsaw puzzle. Usually the movement of the earth is slow, although sometimes a piece moves suddenly and causes an earthquake.

Scientists who study the earth look at rocks, at the way the land is formed, and at the earth's changing magnetic fields. These are a record of what has happened in the past. Fossils also help scientists figure out what the earth might have been like long ago. If similar fossils are found in two different continents, it suggests that the two pieces of land may once have been connected.

Because we know that certain animals lived only at certain times, their fossils help us to determine the age of the rocks in which they were found. Fossils of water-dwelling animals help us to learn when certain parts of the earth were covered with oceans or lakes; those of land-dwelling animals show us when the earth was dry land. The earth's temperature also changed, and by knowing what kinds of animals lived in what kinds of climates, we can learn about the weather in ancient times. As far as we know, the earth is the only planet in our solar system on which there is life, and, as we study the rocks and bones and other remnants of the past, we will learn more about its unique history.

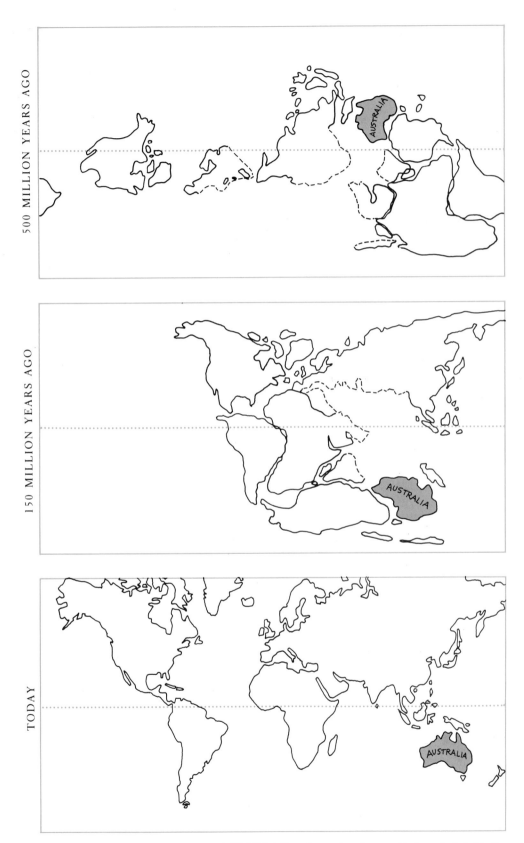

Maps depicting *500 Million Years Ago* and *150 Million Years Ago* are based on graphic forms included in the book *Kadimakara: Extinct Vertebrates* by Pat Rich, Pioneer Design Studio, Victoria, Australia.

# INDEX